A Kid's Guide to
MYTHOLOGY

THOR

TAMMY GAGNE

Mitchell Lane
PUBLISHERS
P.O. Box 196
Hockessin, DE 19707
www.mitchelllane.com

Printing   1   2   3   4   5   6   7   8

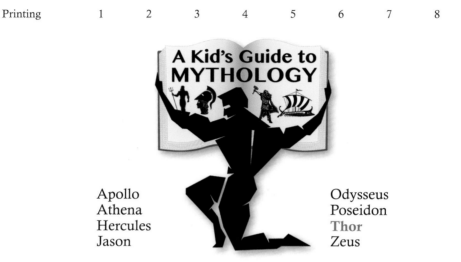

A Kid's Guide to MYTHOLOGY

Apollo
Athena
Hercules
Jason

Odysseus
Poseidon
Thor
Zeus

Library of Congress Cataloging-in-Publication Data
Gagne, Tammy, author.
  Thor / by Tammy Gagne.
     pages cm. — (A kid's guide to mythology)
  Summary: "Chances are good that you have seen the name Thor in a comic book. Or maybe you have seen one of the movies that also bear this famous name. Without a doubt the Norse god of thunder has experienced a surge in popularity in recent years. But he is actually much older than either the men who have played him or the people who have drawn him. Norse mythology came from a group of brutal warriors called the Vikings. As they moved from Scandinavia through Europe, the Vikings shared their stories—the basis for their religion—with others. And along with his father Odin and his rival Loki, Thor became known throughout the rest of the world as well"— Provided by publisher.
  Audience: Ages 8-11.
  Audience: Grades 3-6.
  Includes bibliographical references and index.
  ISBN 978-1-61228-994-6 (library bound)
  1. Thor (Norse deity)—Juvenile literature. 2. Loki (Norse deity)—Juvenile literature.
  3. Mythology, Norse—Juvenile literature. 4. Vikings—Juvenile literature. I. Title.
  BL870.T5G34 2016
  398.2'0948'01—dc23
                                                                                    2015005448
eBook ISBN: 978-1-61228-995-3

PUBLISHER'S NOTE: The Internet sites referenced herein were active as of the publication date. Due to the fleeting nature of some web sites, we cannot guarantee they will all be active when you are reading this book.

To reflect current usage, we have chosen to use the secular era designations BCE ("before the common era") and CE ("of the common era") instead of the traditional designations BC ("before Christ") and AD (anno Domini, "in the year of the Lord").

DISCLAIMER: Many versions of each myth exist today. The author is covering only one version of each story. Other versions may differ in details.

CONTENTS

Words in **bold** throughout can be found in the Glossary.

This statue in Copenhagen, Denmark, shows Thor being pulled through the sky by his two goats. Thor had the ability to eat his goats for dinner and then bring them back to life the next day.

MYTHOLOGY OF THE VIKINGS

"You like comic books?" Jason asked as he plopped down on the grass beside his friend Sophie. She was sitting in the shade of the biggest oak tree at the park. Other kids were rollerblading or playing basketball. But Sophie was glued to the open book in front of her.

"I do," she answered. "But this isn't a comic book. It's one of my favorite graphic novels. They're longer than comic books, with more complex stories. This one is about Thor. Do you like mythology?"

"Thor . . ." Jason said, mostly to himself. He thought he remembered seeing a movie by that name. "Is he a Greek god or a Roman god?"

"Neither," replied Sophie. "He is the **Norse** god of thunder. You've heard of the Vikings, right? Norse myths are their stories."

They Came, and They Conquered
The Vikings were sailors from the Scandinavian lands—Denmark, Norway, and Sweden. They traveled to other parts of Europe, as well as Greenland, North Africa, and the Middle East, between the eighth and eleventh centuries CE. Most Europeans saw the Vikings as brutal pirates. In some ways, this was true. But many parts of the Vikings'

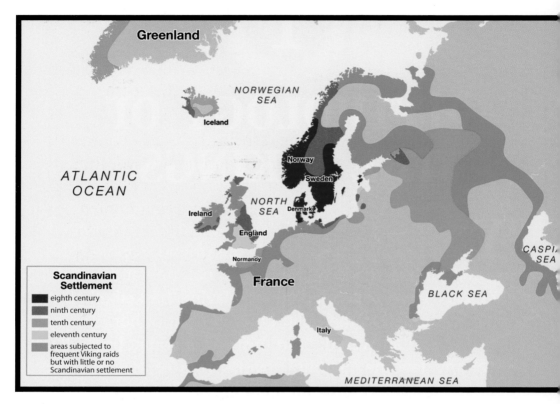

history are misunderstood. The Vikings were far from an organized group. They weren't even a united one.

Archaeologist William Fitzhugh explains, "For the most part, the **raids** were totally independent. They were not the result of national armies or navies moving down into Europe, but rather the actions of individual Viking chieftains who grouped together followers and had one or maybe several boats. Occasionally . . . they organized whole **flotillas** and made a purposeful kind of attack, but generally they were much more individualistic. They had to find food, and they couldn't carry their food with them. They had to live off the land, so they drove people out and took whatever money and other valuables people had."[1]

The Vikings were brutal, however. Fitzhugh points out that they killed many people. But he also notes that violence was common at this time. "I think they were relatively **ruthless**, but remember, this was a ruthless age with far more than just peaceful farmers living peaceful lives. All sorts of things were going on in the **British Isles** and mainland Europe, including constant battles between rival princes vying [competing] for kingship and control of local regions. The Vikings were just another crowd, though a crowd that was non-Christian and had no compunction [regret or guilty feelings] about killing churchmen or women or children." But, Fitzhugh adds, "They weren't out to kill everyone in the countryside but rather to find a way to live."[2]

Giant Tales

Over time the Vikings settled into different regions of Europe. Many of them converted to Christianity. But they didn't forget the religion of their **ancestors**. The Vikings were excellent storytellers. They shared their myths everywhere they went.

Norse mythology stated that long before the world was created, two distinct regions existed. One, called Niflheim (NIV-uhl-heym), was made up of ice, frost, and fog. The other was Muspelheim (MOO-spell-heym). This region was known as the land of fire. Between the two regions was an empty space called Ginnungagap (GIN-oong-gah-GAHP).

In the beginning nothing existed in Ginnungagap. But air spread through this area from one region to the other. Eventually the scorching heat from Muspelheim melted some of the ice in Niflheim. The dripping water began to pool within the empty space. And within it grew a frost giant, or Jotun (YOH-tun). His name was Ymir (EE-mir). Soon several more Jotnar appeared.

And around them, their world called Jotunheim (YOH-tun-heym) was created.

As Ymir and his fellow frost giants emerged from the water, other creatures also came into being. One was a cow giant named Audhumla (OUD-hoom-lah) who gave milk to the frost giants. As Audhumla was licking a salty block of ice one day, she noticed a hair growing out of the ice block. The next day, she licked more, and the hair had become an entire head. And by the third day, the first god was whole. His name was Buri (BOOR-ee). The gods' world, called Asgard (AHS-gahrd), also then came into being.

The gods and the frost giants quickly became bitter enemies. And the giants were beginning to outnumber the gods. Ymir kept creating more and more frost giants like him.

Buri's grandsons hatched a plan to stop Ymir. Odin (OH-din) and his brothers Vili (VIH-lee) and Ve (vee-YAY) waited until the giant was sleeping and proceeded to attack him. It was a bloody fight. But in the end the gods were victorious. The gods transformed the giant's remains into the human world. The Vikings called this new place Midgard (MID-gahrd). Ymir's flesh became the land, his blood the oceans, and his brain the clouds. This is the Norse myth that explained the creation of the world.

Different, but the Same

Some people are quick to compare Norse mythology to the more widely known Greek or Roman stories. For example, you might hear someone say that Odin is the Norse version of the Greek god Zeus. Both Odin and Zeus are the rulers of all the other gods in their separate realms.

Some of the myths from different cultures sound remarkably similar to one another. Rick Riordan is the author of the Percy Jackson book series. The series tells new stories about the children of the Greek gods and goddesses. Riordan shares, "The Aztecs and Sumerians both have stories about the water god destroying the world by flood, saving only one righteous man. The Egyptian god Osiris (oh-SAHY-ris) and the Greek god Dionysus (dah-uh-NAHY-suhs) are both chopped into pieces, only to be put back together and reborn. The Celts and Hindus both tell tales of the gods of light battling the ancient gods of darkness."[3]

All types of mythology have two basic things in common: First, each set of stories was created long ago as a way of explaining nature and other mysteries. When the Greeks looked to

Norse god Odin

the moon, they believed this heavenly body was controlled by a goddess named Artemis (AHR-tuh-mis). Likewise when the Baltic people looked to the sun, they thought that Saule (SOW-lay) was running the incredible light show. When something unusual like an **eclipse** happened, some people believed that an animal or monster was trying to steal the sun or moon.

Riordan admits, "We mortals have always been in awe of the world around us. Even now, in an age of science, we feel powerless when faced with earthquakes and hurricanes. It's no wonder, then, that many ancient cultures came up with stories about mighty gods who got angry at the world."[4]

The second thing most forms of mythology share is that they were—or still are—forms of religion. **Polytheistic** religions are those that teach that many gods exist. Instead of believing that the universe had a single creator, the people of polytheistic societies pray to a different god or goddess, depending on the subject. For instance, an ancient Roman faced with an important decision, might pray to Minerva (mi-NUR-vuh), the Roman goddess of wisdom. A Scandinavian, on the other hand, would look to Mimir (MEE-meer), the Norse god of wisdom, for guidance.

Thor is the Norse god of thunder. Like Sophie, you may have read stories about Thor. Or like Jason, perhaps you have seen a movie about him. But both the graphic novels and the major motion pictures offer only a glimpse into the world of this fascinating character. Most modern versions of Thor's story are also a blending of the actual Norse mythology and the imagination of pop culture.

SOUND FAMILIAR?

Snorri Sturluson was an Icelandic chieftain who lived during the thirteenth century. Much of what we know about Norse mythology comes from his writings. It is unlikely that he made up the Norse myths. But he was the first to write them down. And it is more than likely that he added many details to the stories.

Norse mythology has served as an inspiration for some of the world's most beloved authors. One of the best known of these was J.R.R. Tolkien, who wrote *The Hobbit* and *The Lord of the Rings*. In 2012, Nancy Marie Brown wrote a book about Sturluson. But before she knew who Sturluson was, Tolkien's books introduced her to many of the characters in Norse mythology.

As Brown recalls, "When I was four a babysitter read me *The Hobbit*. My older sister gave me *The Lord of the Rings* when I was thirteen. Through college, Tolkien was my favorite author—even though such 'escapist fiction' was considered inappropriate for an English major to read in the late 1970s. Imagine my delight when I was assigned *The Prose Edda*, by the thirteenth-century Icelandic author Snorri Sturluson, in a class on comparative mythology and began recognizing names out of *The Hobbit*: Bifur, Bofur, Bombur, Nori, Ori, Oin, Gloin . . . even Gandalf. What was Tolkien's wizard doing in medieval Iceland?"[5]

Snorri Sturluson

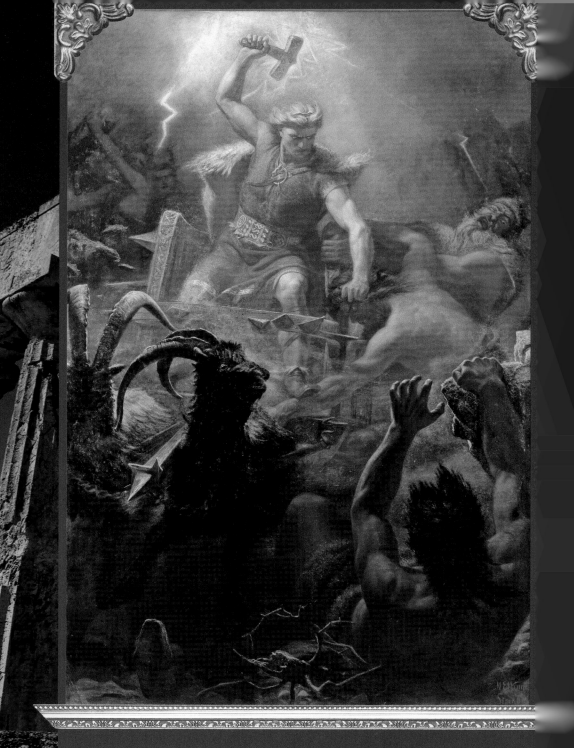

This 1872 painting by Swedish artist Mårten Eskil Winge shows Thor battling the Jotnar with his famous hammer.

ANCIENT HERO, MODERN HEARTTHROB

The Vikings looked up to many of the Norse gods. But none, not even Odin, was as revered as Thor. The frost giants didn't hate the gods alone. They also detested Midgard—and all humans who lived there. The giants tried to destroy human beings at every opportunity. But Thor was always there to protect the people.

The biggest of all the gods, Thor was also brave and strong. He loved a good fight, especially one with giants. He also had two special tools for this purpose. One was his belt, which was said to double his strength. The other was a hammer powerful enough to crush a giant's skull. This incredible weapon even had a name—Mjolnir (MYOHL-neer).

The frost giants feared Thor and his massive hammer. Because of this the Vikings and other Norse people began to view hammers as good luck charms. They carved hammer shapes above the doors of their homes. They believed that the images would make their dwellings safer and stronger. Many Norse people carried small **replicas** of Thor's hammer with them for protection. They even named a day of the week after the Norse god. Hundreds of years later, the fifth day is still called Thursday—originally Thor's Day.

CHAPTER 2

Reinventing a God

Today many people revere Thor as much for his looks as for his actions. In both comics and movies, Thor is almost always depicted as tall, muscular, and clean-shaven with long blond hair. And thanks to actor Chris Hemsworth, many female moviegoers have grown fond of this version of the Norse god. Norse mythology does describe Thor as brawny and brave. But he wasn't blond.

According to writer Rob Bricken, there are quite a few differences between the original Thor and the one portrayed in movies and comic books. He explains that the original Thor "had red hair, was never willingly without his beard, and gloried in battle to the point where Marvel's Thor might have thought him a supervillain."[1]

It is clear that publishers and movie makers have put their own spin on Thor. All the changes have led to many misconceptions about the god. Some pieces of the story have even been lost in the retelling of the tales. "The Norse Thor needed magic gloves to have Mjolnir fly back to him, and a special belt to use Mjolnir at its full power," notes Bricken. "While Marvel used the belt in the alternative universe *Ultimates* comics, the gloves have not been mentioned in the regular Marvel [Universe] at all."[2]

It seems that some parts of the story have been left out for the sake of romance. In the comics and movies, for example, Thor's only love is a human named Jane Foster. But the myths tell the story a little differently. In Norse mythology Thor takes a wife in his own world when he marries a goddess by the name of Sif (SEEF).

Original Details

The original tales tell of a god who flies through the sky with a **chariot** pulled by two goats. Humans could hear the rumbling of the vehicle's huge iron wheels. They

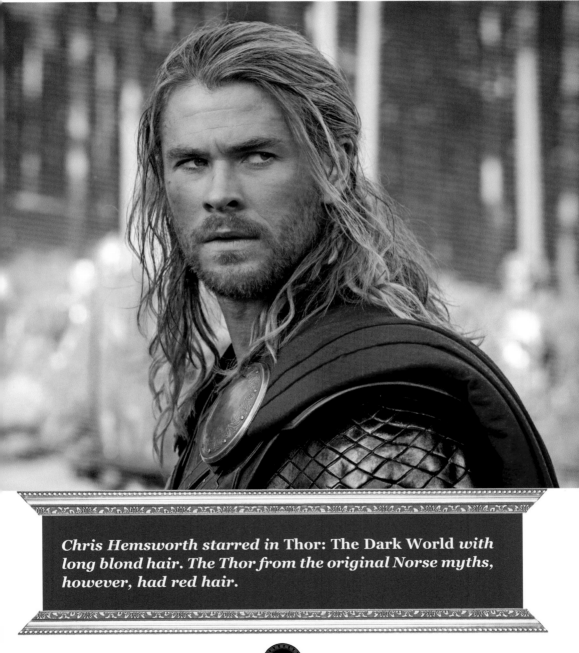

Chris Hemsworth starred in Thor: The Dark World *with long blond hair. The Thor from the original Norse myths, however, had red hair.*

called the sound thunder. And to them, the sparks flying from the wheels were lightning. Before humans in Midgard would set out on long trips, they would pray to Thor for good weather.

The Thor of Norse mythology was undeniably larger than life. But he did have his limitations. For instance, he could only fly with the help of his magical goats. But the goats have barely made it into the modern versions of Thor's story. Instead, the Thor we read about in graphic novels or watch from the front-row at a movie theater appears to fly just by throwing his hammer and hanging on to it.

Modern books and films have also made changes to Thor's father, Odin. In the 2011 film *Thor*, Odin's character is highly focused on peace. Odin from Norse mythology was very different. "Odin loves war," shares Bricken, "and he loves starting fights—contrast that to Anthony Hopkins's Odin in the *Thor* movie, where he banishes Thor for picking merely a fight with the frost giants. Also, the original Odin was not exactly a beloved **deity** as much as a god to be feared."[3]

While it's true that comic books, graphic novels, and movies have made some mistakes, they have also accomplished something positive. These popular genres have brought Thor and his fellow Norse gods to life for the modern masses. Before Marvel introduced Thor in its comic books in 1962, few kids knew much about Thor at all. Since that time, Thor has gone from an ancient hero to a household name.

A Modern Twist

The editors and writers at Marvel Comics aren't the only ones who have reinvented Thor and his fellow Norse gods in modern fiction. Francesca Simon, author of the popular *Horrid Henry* book series, has written a children's novel called *The Lost Gods*. In it Odin, Thor, and the goddess Freya (FREY-uh) have lost their powers. They come to London in hopes of regaining them. As writer S.F. Said describes the story, "They need more worshippers to regain their strength and defeat the Frost Giants. At first, it goes badly. Their lordly demands to be worshipped are politely ignored at best." Most people assume they are crazy. But placing the ancient gods in the modern world produces some funny situations. "When Thor demands 'A horn of shining ale!' he is offered lemonade. The gods see [a billboard] of David Beckham in his underwear and declare him divine [godly]; they think an Apple store must be a modern temple."[4]

While humorous, the book points out some of the ways the world has changed. Odin notices that many people in modern society worship famous people instead of the gods. In one scene Odin is told that if he wishes to win fans, he must have a Twitter account and learn to tweet. "Though he is scornful, [Odin] eventually gets more followers than Lady Gaga." And "Freya, goddess of beauty, initially dismissed as 'too fat,' ends up reshaping the fashion industry in her image."[5]

This Stockholm, Sweden, statue shows Freya with a falcon perched on her hand. When she wore a coat made of falcon feathers, Freya could fly.

Thor's mother, Jord, is both a Jotun and a symbol of Earth. This statue shows her as a loving mother.

3

THE WORLD OF THOR

It is difficult to admire Thor without also having a healthy respect for the frost giants. For one thing, Thor is related to these creatures he has become famous for fighting. Thor's mother Jord (YORD) was a Jotun. Some say that Thor must have received his overpowering strength from his mother.

In the movies Frigga (FREE-guh) is Thor's mother. But this character, called simply Frigg in Norse mythology, is actually Thor's stepmother. Whenever stories are told and retold over centuries, there is bound to be some confusion. But Thor's stories contain more variations than most. Even Rene Russo, who plays Frigga in the films, isn't completely certain of her relationship to her supposed son. But she clearly has a good sense of humor about it. "I am so confused," she admitted in an interview. "Is Thor my son or not? People have been telling me recently, 'No, you're not his mother.' It's all so confusing! I got to tell ya, it would be a little embarrassing if I don't know. I need to read more about her."[1]

Even in the Norse myths, little information is given about Jord. She is described simply as the daughter of Nott and Annarr. Some people have suggested that since Jord means "Earth," it may not be the actual name of Thor's mother. Author Dan McCoy explains, "In all likelihood, what the passages are really saying is that Thor is the son of *an* earth goddess, but not necessarily any one specific earth goddess. 'Earth' here seems to be more of a general concept than a discrete figure."[2]

Although Odin has a child with Jord, he eventually ends up marrying Frigg instead. Unlike Jord, Frigg is one of the Aesir (EY-sir), the name of the group of gods that Odin and Thor belong to. Regardless of his heritage, Thor does not feel a connection to the frost giants.

The Family Troublemaker

The best known trickster from Jotunheim is Loki (LOH-kee). But this frost giant isn't like the others. For starters, he is a shape shifter, able to change his physical form when necessary. He is also handsome and capable of being impressively charming when he wants to be. In the Norse myths, Loki came to live in Asgard when he was a young Jotun. He joined Odin's family as his brother by choice. Modern movies and comic books cast Loki as Thor's adopted sibling instead.

Regardless of where Loki fits into the gods' family tree, the clever Jotun becomes a god of mischief in Asgard. He possesses a great talent for saving the day—when he wants to. It is also important to note that Loki creates a great number of the problems he helps solve.

In one story Thor's wife Sif awoke to find that Loki had cut off her long, beautiful hair. Loki knew how much Sif valued her long, gorgeous locks. And he knew that Thor loved them as well. When Thor found out what Loki had done, he declared that he would kill him for it. But Odin would not allow it. "Nay, not so, Thor," he said. "Nay,

Thor's wife Sif was known for her flowing golden hair, illustrated here by British artist John Charles Dollman.

no Dweller in Asgard may slay another. I shall summon Loki to come before us here. It is for you to make him (and remember that Loki is cunning and able to do many things) bring back to Sif the beauty of her golden hair."[3]

But it was Odin who ordered the Jotun to fix what he had done. As was Loki's way, he did so through mischief. He turned to the dwarfs of Svartalfheim (SVART-alf-heym),

In this picture, Loki is on the run, trying to escape punishment. After getting himself into trouble, he ran from Asgard and hid out in a hut near a waterfall. During the day he turned into a fish to remain out of sight, and at night he crafted a fishing net to catch food. However when the gods found Loki's hiding place, Loki— as a fish—had to escape his own invention. Thor eventually caught Loki as he jumped through the air, and brought the trickster to face his punishment.

which was located below the earth. Knowing their ability to beat metal into a variety of different shapes, he began by **flattering** them. But it was going to take more than compliments to get them to do what he needed. Like the frost giants, the dwarfs were envious of the gods. They longed for the riches of Asgard, so that is what Loki promised them in exchange for their help.

"Have you got a bar of fine gold that you can hammer into threads—into threads so fine that they will be like the hair of Sif, Thor's wife?" he asked. "Only the Dwarfs could make a thing so wonderful. Ah, there is the bar of gold. Hammer it into those fine threads, and the Gods themselves will be jealous of your work," he assured them.[4]

According to the myth, the results were spectacular. "The threads were as bright as sunlight, and when Loki took up the mass of worked gold it flowed from his raised hand down on the ground. It was so fine that it could be put into his palm, and it was so light that a bird might not feel its weight."[5] When Loki returned to lay the shining new locks on Sif's head, the other gods and goddesses cheered at the wondrous sight. Loki had saved the day— and avoided Thor's **vengeance**.

In the *Thor* movies, the role of Loki is played by actor Tom Hiddleston. "Like Hiddleston's version of the character," writes journalist Lily Rothman, "the mythological Loki is a complicated guy, whose **allegiances** are hard to pin down—but the similarities are pretty limited after that. . . . While in early stages of Loki's story [in Norse mythology] he's more mischievous than straight-up bad, his transition from **puckish** to evil takes place over time."[6]

Actor Tom Hiddleston plays Loki in the Marvel Studios films about Thor and the other Norse gods.

FAMILY FEUD

In Norse mythology Thor has several half-siblings. Balder (BAWL-der) was said to be the most beautiful and kindest god in all of Asgard. He lived under a roof made of silver. Giant pillars of gold held up the dwelling. It was so magnificent that no evil could take place within it. If that was the case, his death must have taken place somewhere else. But we know that it came at the hands of Thor's other half-brother, Hoder. Loki tricked the blind god, guiding him to shoot Balder dead with an arrow made from mistletoe.

Frigg sent her son Hermod (HER-mood) to the **underworld** to beg for his sibling's return. Hel, the goddess of death, agreed to let Balder return to Asgard. But she insisted on one condition: Every living and dead thing had to weep for him. If even a single one did not, he would stay. All wept for the god except one giantess, who was actually Loki in disguise. Balder would remain with Hel.

Perhaps Frigg should have sent Tyr (TEER) instead. He was known as the bravest of the gods. Or she might have asked Bragi (BRAH-gee). This half-sibling to Thor was known for his wisdom and his way with words. Maybe he could have convinced Hel to release his beloved brother without any strings.

Thor may be the strongest of all the Norse gods. But his half-brother, Tyr, is known as the bravest god.

In addition to his hammer, it was said that Thor had a crown of bright, shining stars.

4

PERFECT IMPERFECTIONS

Thor is a fascinating character because he is known both for his strengths and for his faults. He isn't interested in causing mischief like Loki. But Thor is far from perfect himself. In addition to being brave and strong, Thor is also arrogant, stubborn, and hot tempered.

The films have stayed true to this part of Thor's personality. In the 2011 movie *Thor*, he picks a fight with the frost giants. A disappointed Odin then punishes him by sending him to Midgard to live among the humans. "Through your arrogance and stupidity," Odin declares, "you've opened these peaceful realms and innocent lives to the horror and desolation of war! You are unworthy of these realms, you're unworthy of your title, you're unworthy of the loved ones you have betrayed. I now take from you your power! In the name of my father and his father before, I, Odin Allfather, cast you out!"[1]

This particular event never happened in any of the ancient myths. But it includes a detail that some critics see as a brilliant addition. From the time comic book creator Stan Lee turned Thor into a Marvel hero, only the god himself could lift his mighty hammer. But when Odin casts him out, Thor loses this special ability. Only someone deserving of the weapon will be blessed with the privilege of being able to lift it—and use it. "Whosoever holds this hammer, if he be worthy, shall possess the power of Thor!" announces Odin.[2]

Powerful but Not Perfect

Norse myth explains that Thor's trademark hammer was created as a result of Loki's mischief. When Loki brought back Sif's golden hair, he also brought a spear for Odin and a ship that could be folded up and carried in a pocket. Loki was so proud of the dwarfs' creations that he bet two other dwarfs that they could not make anything better. The dwarfs won the bet when they crafted Mjolnir. The hammer was promised to never miss its target. And after it was used, it would always return to its owner, much like a boomerang. The gift excited the gods, who knew it would be useful in their battles against the frost giants.

Indeed, the hammer proved to be as powerful as promised. Thor, on the other hand, had his share of weaknesses despite his physical strength. One of those weaknesses was that he could be tricked by magic.

In one story Thor and Loki traveled through Jotunheim with two servants. They were headed toward the city of Utgard (OOT-gahrd), where Thor planned to have some fun by challenging the giants to a competition. Along the way they found a large house that looked like a safe place to stay for the night. But the dwelling proved to be anything but peaceful. Loud noises shook the floor as they tried to sleep. In the morning they came out of the house and saw a sleeping giant, shaking the ground as he snored. The giant awoke and told Thor and Loki that his name was Skrymir (SKREE-mir). In the light of day, they could now see that the "house" was actually the giant's glove.

Thor is indeed the strongest god. But he often fell victim to magic and tricks, like the ones that the giant Skrymir played on him.

Skrymir offered to help Thor and his companions. He would walk with them, carrying a heavy sack of supplies and food through the mountains. After traveling a long distance, the giant was tired, but not hungry. He told Thor and the others to take food from his sack so they could eat while he slept. But the sack was tied up with so many knots that Thor could not open it. As he struggled with the bag, he grew angry. He was certain that Skrymir had made the sack impossible to open on purpose. As the giant lay sleeping, Thor threw his hammer at his forehead. The weapon should have killed Skrymir. But he barely noticed. Instead, the giant merely stirred, asking if a leaf had fallen on him while he slept.

An even angrier Thor then hurled the hammer at the sleeping giant once more. This time, Skrymir looked around for the acorn that had fallen on him. Not understanding how his hammer could be failing him, Thor delivered a third and final blow with all his strength. And what did the giant think had hit him? Bird droppings!

The next day Skrymir left the group, pointing Thor and the others in the direction of Utgard. When they arrived, they learned that the king of the giants had been expecting them. He had arranged several contests to test the skills of the travelers against those of the giants. Loki wasted no time in bragging about how much food he could eat. And he backed up his claims by choking down several platters of meat. But his competitor Logi (LAW-gee) ate the same amount of meat, and he ate the bones and the table too!

One of Thor's servants also faced a challenge. In his case it was a contest of speed. Like Loki, the servant had boasted about his abilities. He claimed to be as fast as lightning. But when they raced, the servant was easily beaten by the giant Hugi (HYOO-gee).

Next Thor insisted that he could drink more than any being alive. Like the others, though, he could not back up his boastfulness. He drank and drank. But the liquid in the drinking horn barely decreased.

Thor and the others went to bed and planned to leave early the next morning. They were too embarrassed to face their opponents again. But as the group tried to leave, they were met by the king. He invited them to have breakfast before they set out. The king admitted that he had tricked Thor and his companions. On their journey, he had disguised himself as Skrymir. When Thor tried to hit the king with his hammer, "Skrymir" had used magic to put a hill where his head was. Loki's competitor in the eating contest wasn't a giant after all. Instead, his challenger had been fire, which destroys everything in its path. The servant's competitor in the foot race had been thought. Nothing moves faster than the speed of thought. And Thor's drinking horn had been connected to the sea so that it could never be emptied.

Drinking horn

THE LAND OF FIRE AND ICE

The settings for the Norse myths are remarkably similar to the native lands of the Vikings. Iceland, for example, has much in common with the frigid world of Niflheim. The modern nation is home to many large icy glaciers. But in other ways Iceland is also like Muspelheim. Magma flows beneath the ground, exploding and forming volcanoes. The magma also heats nearby underground water, which can boil and expand. This results in a bubbling hot water explosion above the surface of the earth, called a geyser. One of Iceland's most famous geysers, called Strokkur (STRAH-kur), erupts every five minutes or so. Because of Iceland's extreme conditions, people often call it the land of fire and ice.

Strokkur Geyser in southwest Iceland.

The island nation of Iceland has an unusually large number of active volcanoes.

Thor and Loki may be enemies sometimes, but they often work together. Here, the duo sets off on a journey to Jotunheim in Thor's chariot.

5

FAMOUS FRENEMIES

A fair number of stories depict Thor and Loki as enemies. But in many instances—in both myths and movies—they work together for a common goal. Even under the best of circumstances, however, a spirited competition exists between them. At times the **banter** seems playful, while at others it has a darker quality. In the film *Thor: The Dark World*, Thor calls on Loki in his jail cell.

Loki is less than welcoming. "Thor. After all this time and now you come to visit me. Why? Have you come to **gloat**? To mock?" he asks. Thor explains that he needs his brother's help, but he knows that he can't trust Loki. "You betray me, and I will kill you," Thor warns.[1]

Once Loki agrees to help, Thor breaks him out of jail. The pair then takes off in an aircraft in search of Thor's latest enemy. As Thor navigates through the sky hitting buildings along the way, Loki suggests, "Look, why don't you let me take over? I'm clearly the better pilot!"[2]

"Is that right?" Thor responds. "Well, out of the two of us, which one can actually fly?"[3] Of course, we know that the Thor of Norse mythology could not in fact fly. But Thor's attitude toward Loki is true to the old stories. While Loki is usually cast as the villain, the rivalry between the two was indeed two-sided.

Joining Forces

Like the movies, the old Norse myths also include stories in which Thor and Loki work together. In one of them, Loki helps Thor retrieve his hammer from a giant named Thrym (THRIM). The pair visited Freya to borrow her magic feathered coat, which gave its wearer the ability to fly. Loki put on the coat and flew to Jotunheim to find Thrym.

When he found Thrym, Loki immediately began questioning him. Finally, Thrym admitted that it was indeed he who stole the hammer. He and his fellow giants feared the weapon greatly. But now it couldn't hurt them. Thrym then explained to Loki that he had buried Mjolnir eight miles beneath the ground. "No one can win it back from me, unless he brings to me fair Freya as a bride," the giant insisted.[4]

Loki flew back to Asgard where Thor was waiting for news. "Were your labors successful?" he asked.[5]

Loki explained the giant's demands and the pair set off to deliver Freya to Jotunheim. The goddess had been happy to lend her magic coat to help Thor reclaim his hammer, but she was not willing to marry a giant. Despite Thor's insistence, she refused. The other gods and goddesses agreed that Thor and Loki were asking too much of Freya. But the hammer was important for the protection of all the gods, and the humans, too. There had to be another way to get the hammer back.

After some thought, the future-seeing god Heimdall (HEYM-dahl) noted that since it was Thor's hammer, he should be the one to get it back. The god suggested that Thor dress up in bridal clothes and go to the giant in Freya's place. Now that he was the one who would have to "marry" the giant, Thor wasn't very excited. "What! I dress in women's garb?" he yelled. "I—I wear a garland of flowers?"[6]

Despite his resistance, Thor traveled to Jotunheim dressed as the bride. Loki joined him as a bridesmaid. They wore veils over their faces so the giants would not

Loki wears Freya's coat of feathers to pay a visit to the giant Thrym. After some questioning, Thrym finally admits to stealing Thor's hammer.

recognize them. Once there, they joined the wedding party that Thrym and the other giants had prepared. It was a wedding custom at this time for the groom to place a hammer in the bride's lap at the ceremony. When Thrym brought out Mjolnir, Thor made his move. He killed Thrym and all the other giants in the room. Thor finally had his hammer back.

After filming *Thor: The Dark World*, Chris Hemsworth shared his thoughts on the relationship between Thor and Loki. "I think in the comic books you kind of roll your eyes sometimes at the amount of times they're back to being best friends. And so we wanted to keep in mind, Loki did just try to kill you for the seventh time—and Earth."[7]

But in *The Avengers*, the mood between the pair is somewhat lighter. Hemsworth also appreciates the simpler side of the characters. "It's what I loved about the comics," he shares. "It was never clean and cut and that's it. It was always like, Thor would forgive him, they'd be friends, and Loki would betray him again. 'You idiot, Thor! Again?' But it was different than your normal good guy, bad guy scenario. They're brothers, you know? Anyone with siblings understands that. 'That's it, I'm never talking to you again . . . want to play football?'"[8]

Fulfilling Their Destiny

The stories of the Norse gods, giants, and dwarfs don't just take place in the past. Norse mythology also describes Ragnarok, a battle which will happen in the future. Before this battle takes place, there will be three years of winter— no spring, summer, or fall. The gods know this final battle is coming, and they know that most of them will die in it. There is nothing they can do to stop it. Still, the gods,

The beginning of Ragnarok is shown in this 1908 image. Ragnarok was not just an ending, though. It also represented a new beginning.

giants, humans, and other beings will not go down without giving the battle their all.

This final battle will not be without its victories. In a past story, Thor had tried to slay the Midgard **serpent**. This gigantic creature lived in the ocean, and was so large that it surrounded the earth. Thor had once managed to catch the serpent with a fishing pole, using an ox's head as bait. But a giant named Hymir (HEE-mir) cut the line at the last minute. Thor punished the giant by drowning him. But the serpent had already gotten away. During Ragnarok,

Thor battles and kills the Midgard serpent. Those who believed in the Norse god realized that despite his strength, Thor could and would eventually die.

though, Thor will finally manage to slay the beast, but then will only be able to walk nine steps before the serpent's **venom** kills him.

Loki joins his adopted family in this final battle, but he too will perish in the fight. Odin will be swallowed by the wolf Fenrir (FEN-rir). At the battle's end, the giant Surt will create a fire that spreads through all the worlds, destroying almost everything. Even the land that arose out of nothing will sink into nothingness once more. What seems to be the end of the world, however, is really just a rebirth. Despite all the destruction, a few will survive, including two humans. From them, the world will begin again. And the stories of Thor and his fellow gods will continue to live on for eternity.

More Than a Story

Most people think of the Norse myths as merely old stories. But they are also the basis for a present-day religion. In a letter to the editor of London's *Daily Mail* newspaper, reader Claire Jordan points out, "The worship of the Aesir, the Norse **pantheon**, isn't a dead mythology, but a still living religion, especially in Iceland."[9]

Known as Odinism, the religion has a definite following in Europe, Australia, and the Americas. People who practice Odinism do not view the Norse gods as fictional characters. Instead, they believe the Norse gods are actual supreme beings with special powers. They pray to these gods as followers of other religions pray to their own gods. And like those other gods, Odinists believe the Norse gods are capable of answering their prayers.

Odinists respect the Norse gods immensely. But they don't see the gods as superior to humans. They do not kneel or bow down when praying, for example. Instead, they stand tall, because they believe they are worthy of the gods' respect as well. The Odinist Fellowship website states, "Odinists regard our gods, not as our masters, but as firm friends and powerful **allies**."[10]

Much like Odinism, Asatru is a religion that is based on traditional Norse beliefs. Here, a group of Asatru followers gather to participate in a ceremony for the holiday of Sigurblot, which marks the first day of summer.

CHAPTER NOTES

Chapter 1: Mythology of the Vikings

1. William Fitzhugh, interview by Julia Cort, "Who Were the Vikings?" PBS, *NOVA*, February 8, 2005, http://www.pbs.org/wgbh/nova/ancient/who-were-vikings.html

2. Ibid.

3. Rick Riordan, "Mysteries of Gods and Myths," *Times* (London), October 5, 2011.

4. Ibid.

5. Nancy Marie Brown, interview by Peter Konieczny, "Interview: *Song of the Vikings: Snorri and the Making of Norse Myths*," Medievalists.net, December 13, 2012, http://www.medievalists.net/2012/12/13/interview-song-of-the-vikings-snorri-and-the-making-of-norse-myths/

Chapter 2: Ancient Hero, Modern Heartthrob

1. Rob Bricken, "8 Things Marvel Got Wrong About Thor and Norse Mythology," io9, November 5, 2013, http://io9.com/8-things-marvel-got-wrong-about-thor-and-norse-mytholog-1458989921

2. Ibid.

3. Ibid.

4. S.F. Said, "The Lost Gods, Review—A Mythical Romp from the Horrid Henry Author," *Guardian*, March 22, 2014, http://www.theguardian.com/books/2014/mar/22/lost-gods-review-francesa-simon-horrid-henry-author

5. Ibid.

Chapter 3: The World of Thor

1. Jennifer Vineyard, "Rene Russo Wants to Brush Up on Her Comic-Book History Before *Thor* 2," Vulture.com, July 31, 2012, http://www.vulture.com/2012/07/rene-russo-wants-to-brush-up-before-thor-2.html

2. Dan McCoy, "Jord," Norse Mythology for Smart People, http://norse-mythology.org/jord/

3. Padraic Colum, *The Children of Odin* (Boston, MA: Digireads.com, 2008), p. 29.

42

CHAPTER NOTES

4. Ibid., p. 32.

5. Ibid.

6. Lily Rothman, "The 'Truth' about Thor and Loki," *Time*, November 8, 2013, http://entertainment.time.com/2013/11/08/the-truth-about-thor-and-loki/

Chapter 4: Perfect Imperfections

1. *Thor*, directed by Kenneth Branagh (Hollywood, CA: Paramount Pictures, 2011), DVD.

2. Ibid.

Chapter 5: Famous Frenemies

1. *Thor: The Dark World*, directed by Alan Taylor (Burbank, CA: Walt Disney Studios, 2013), DVD.

2. Ibid.

3. Ibid.

4. D.L. Ashliman, ed., "The Lay of Thrym," *Poetic Edda*, 2009, http://www.pitt.edu/~dash/thrym.html

5. Ibid.

6. Colum, *The Children of Odin*, p. 120.

7. Rob Keyes, "'Thor: The Dark World' Set Interview with Chris Hemsworth," ScreenRant, http://screenrant.com/thor-2-chris-hemsworth-set-interview/

8. Joey Paur, "Chris Hemsworth Talks About Thor and Loki's Relationship in Thor 2," GeekTyrant.com, http://geektyrant.com/news/2012/5/16/chris-hemsworth-talks-about-thor-and-lokis-relationship-in-t.html

9. Claire M. Jordan, "Living Legends: Letters," *Daily Mail*, April 15, 2014.

10. Odinist Fellowship, "All About Odinism . . . Your Questions Answered," http://www.odinistfellowship.co.uk/

WORKS CONSULTED

Ashliman, D.L., editor. "The Lay of Thrym." *Poetic Edda*. 2009. http://www.pitt.edu/~dash/thrym.html

Bennington Banner. "Nancy Marie Brown's 'Song of the Vikings.'" November 24, 2012. http://www.benningtonbanner.com/artsweekend/ci_22056443/nancy-marie-browns-lsquo-song-vikings

Billson, Anne. "Cutter's Way and the Great Tradition of the Film Eyepatch." *Guardian*, June 23, 2011. http://www.theguardian.com/film/2011/jun/23/film-eyepatch-tradition

Bricken, Rob. "8 Things Marvel Got Wrong About Thor and Norse Mythology." io9, November 5, 2013. http://io9.com/8-things-marvel-got-wrong-about-thor-and-norse-mytholog-1458989921

Brown, Nancy Marie. Interview by Peter Konieczny. "Interview: *Song of the Vikings: Snorri and the Making of Norse Myths*." Medievalists.net, December 13, 2012. http://www.medievalists.net/2012/12/13/interview-song-of-the-vikings-snorri-and-the-making-of-norse-myths/

Colum, Padraic. *The Children of Odin*. Boston, MA: Digireads.com, 2008.

Dirda, Michael. "A Scholar Attempts a Tour D'horizon of the Great Mythological Systems of Europe." *Washington Post*, August 17, 2003.

Fitzhugh, William. Interview by Julia Cort. "Who Were the Vikings?" PBS, *NOVA*, February 8, 2005. http://www.pbs.org/wgbh/nova/ancient/who-were-vikings.html

Garry, Jane, and Hasan El-Shamy, editors. *Archetypes and Motifs in Folklore and Literature*. Oxford: Routledge, 2004.

Hamilton, Edith. *Mythology: Timeless Tales of Gods and Heroes*. New York: Grand Central Publishing, 2011.

Jordan, Claire M. "Living Legends: Letters." *Daily Mail*, April 15, 2014.

Keyes, Rob. "'Thor: The Dark World' Set Interview with Chris Hemsworth." ScreenRant. http://screenrant.com/thor-2-chris-hemsworth-set-interview/

McCoy, Dan. "Jord." Norse Mythology for Smart People. http://norse-mythology.org/jord/

WORKS CONSULTED

Odinist Fellowship. "All About Odinism . . . Your Questions Answered." http://www.odinistfellowship.co.uk/

Paur, Joey. "Chris Hemsworth Talks About Thor and Loki's Relationship in Thor 2." GeekTyrant.com. http://geektyrant. com/news/2012/5/16/chris-hemsworth-talks-about-thor-and-lokis-relationship-in-t.html

Philip, Neil. *The Illustrated Book of Myths*. New York: DK Publishing, Inc., 1995.

Riordan, Rick. "Mysteries of Gods and Myths." *Times* (London), October 5, 2011.

Rothman, Lily. "The 'Truth' about Thor and Loki." *Time*, November 8, 2013. http://entertainment.time. com/2013/11/08/the-truth-about-thor-and-loki/

Said, S.F. "The Lost Gods, Review—A Mythical Romp from the Horrid Henry Author." *Guardian*, March 22, 2014. http:// www.theguardian.com/books/2014/mar/22/lost-gods-review-francesa-simon-horrid-henry-author

Thor. Directed by Kenneth Branagh. Hollywood, CA: Paramount Pictures, 2011. DVD.

Thor: The Dark World. Directed by Alan Taylor. Burbank, CA: Walt Disney Studios, 2013. DVD.

Vineyard, Jennifer. "Rene Russo Wants to Brush Up on Her Comic-Book History Before *Thor* 2." Vulture.com, July 31, 2012. http://www.vulture.com/2012/07/rene-russo-wants-to-brush-up-before-thor-2.html

FURTHER READING

Colum, Padraic. *The Children of Odin: The Book of Northern Myths*. New York: Aladdin, 2004.

Lunge-Larsen, Lise. *The Adventures of Thor: The Thunder God*. New York: Houghton Mifflin Company, 2007.

Thomas, Rich. *The Mighty Thor: An Origin Story*. New York: Marvel, 2011.

Williams, Brian. *Understanding Norse Myths*. New York: Crabtree Publishing, 2013.

GLOSSARY

allegiance (uh-LEE-juhns)—devotion or loyalty to a person, group, or cause

ally (AL-ahy)—a person who works together with another for a purpose

ancestor (AN-ses-ter)—a family member from whom a person descends, as a grandparent, great-grandparent, etc.

banter (BAN-ter)—good-natured teasing or joking

British Isles (BRIT-ish AHYLZ)—the islands of Great Britain and Ireland, as well as the smaller islands within the United Kingdom

chariot (CHAR-ee-uht)—an ancient two-wheeled vehicle pulled by animals

deity (DEE-i-tee)—a god or goddess

eclipse (ih-KLIPS)—the total or partial hiding of the sun or moon by the sun, moon, Earth, or other planet

flatter (FLAT-er)—to praise or compliment a lot, or without meaning it

flotilla (floh-TIL-uh)—a group of small ships moving together

gloat (GLOHT)—to be happy about and focused on the misfortune of another, or one's own success at the expense of another

Norse (NAWRS)—related to the Nordic region which includes the modern-day Scandinavian countries (Denmark, Norway, and Sweden), as well as Finland, Iceland, Greenland, the Faroe Islands, and the Aland Islands

pantheon (PAN-thee-on)—the group of gods of a particular mythology, such as the Norse gods or the Greek gods

polytheistic (pol-ee-thee-IS-tik)—believing in or worshipping more than one god

puckish (PUHK-ish)—mischievous

raid (REYD)—a sudden attack or invasion

replica (REP-li-kuh)—a close copy

ruthless (ROOTH-lis)—having no pity; merciless or cruel

serpent (SUR-puhnt)—a large snake

underworld (UHN-der-wurld)—a mythological place where the souls of the dead stay

vengeance (VEN-juhns)—causing harm in return for an injury or offense

venom (VEN-uhm)—the poisonous liquid that some animals produce to harm or kill their victims

INDEX

ABOUT THE AUTHOR

Tammy Gagne is the author of numerous books for adults and children, including *Athena* and *Apollo* for Mitchell Lane Publishers. She resides in northern New England with her husband and son. One of her favorite pastimes is visiting schools to speak to kids about the writing process.